T0193694

# Journey to
# Future Events

Volume 1

James McClain

WESTBOW
PRESS®
A DIVISION OF THOMAS NELSON
& ZONDERVAN

WestBow Press books may be ordered through booksellers or by contacting:

WestBow Press
A Division of Thomas Nelson & Zondervan
1663 Liberty Drive
Bloomington, IN 47403
www.westbowpress.com
1 (866) 928-1240

ISBN: 978-1-9736-6691-2 (sc)
ISBN: 978-1-9736-6692-9 (hc)
ISBN: 978-1-9736-6690-5 (e)

Library of Congress Control Number: 2019909572

Print information available on the last page.

WestBow Press rev. date: 7/16/2019

I would like to thank my wife, Michelle, for being very supportive of my passion to study biblical end-time events. This includes all the work going into the video series and the work going into this book. She has persevered through the many hours I have spent reading, researching, and writing each month's manuscript. You are very understanding, loving, and caring. I love you.

I wish to dedicate this book to my grandfather, the Reverend Charles F. Golden (1887–1963). He was a major influence in my life as I grew up. He was a pastor for forty-three years. I remember spending a lot of time at his home, helping on the farm and going fishing with him. I remember a number of people saying that Reverend Golden was the Billy Graham of his day. I look forward to being in heaven with him. Many times during the hours put into the videos and this book, I have thought of you, Grandpa.

"Even when I am old and gray, do not forsake me, my God, till I declare your power to the next generation, your mighty acts to all who are to come."
—Psalm 71:18

"He said to them, go into all the world and preach the gospel to all creation."
—Mark 16:15

"You must speak my words to them, whether they listen or fail to listen, for they are rebellious."
—Ezekiel 2:7

# Contents

# Preface

This book has been in the making for a number of years. It is the result of accumulating a series of manuscripts used in the production of monthly videos placed on the website journeytofutureevents.com. It was determined that after two years, twenty-four of the manuscripts would be placed in this book.

This book may be used as a standalone read, or you can coordinate this book with the videos located on the website.

These manuscripts are biblically based and the topics chosen by the author. Each topic is related to end-time events as spelled out in the Bible. The desire is that readers will find interest in the topics discussed, dig deeper for their own understanding, and come to the place where they will have a true relationship with God through His Son, Jesus.

There is only one way to eternal life in heaven and that is through Jesus.

# 1

## Chapter

# Christian Eschatology

Welcome to *Journey to Future Events, Volume 1*. In this book I present historical and current world events and discuss the future events the Bible says will occur in the end times.

There are two key principles that must be laid out and explained before we jump into the exciting world of eschatology. These principles are critical to helping you understand the future topics I will be discussing.

The first principle is *knowing God of the Bible*. This will be discussed in chapter 2.

The second principle is *the Bible is God's Word*. This will be discussed in chapter 3.

If you know the God of the Bible, He will enlighten you and give you understanding as you dig into his Word.

The bottom line is this—I want you to have a personal relationship with God. Each of us during our lifetime must either accept or reject the God of the Bible. The Bible is very clear that if you accept God's Son, Jesus, as Lord and Savior, you will live eternally.

So let's jump in. What is Christian eschatology? It is the study of what the Bible says is going to happen in the end times.

The word *eschatology* comes from two Greek words meaning "last" and "study." It is the study of the destiny of humankind as it is revealed in the Bible. It can be the end of an individual life, the end of the age, or the end of the world as we know it.

Did you know that more than a quarter of the Bible is prophecy? More than two thousand prophecies have already been fulfilled. It is estimated that five hundred prophecies remain to be fulfilled.

Please know that no person can know the dates and times of the end-time events—only God knows. If you believe in God and His Word, then what is found in the Bible regarding the end times will happen.

The scripture encourages us to search the Word to determine the nature of things to come.

Revelation 1:3 reads, "Blessed is the one who reads aloud the words of this prophecy, and blessed are those who hear it and take to heart what is written in it, because the time is near."

God also promises this: As we approach the end times, prophecy will become clearer. We see this happening in so many ways in today's world.

What is the real purpose of eschatology? It is to glorify God.

Eschatology helps us to understand the Bible's prophetic passages and how to live our lives in response to what God is going to do in the end times.

Why study eschatology? How is it going to help you and me? Let's review a couple of reasons.

Prophecy is an amazing apologetic, which is simply defined as the defense of the Christian faith.

It is one of the best evangelistic tools today.

If rightly taught, it is a motivator to do good and have a ready heart.

It teaches the church.

It helps us worship God.

It helps us serve with zeal.

It gives us hope in the midst of trouble.

It helps us look forward to heaven.

And it helps us prepare for judgment. Each of us will be judged by God at some point.

# 2

## Chapter

# God of the Bible

*God of the Bible* is one of two very key principles to discuss prior to jumping into future events. Chapter 3 will address the other key principle and is titled "The Bible Is God's Word."

Why these two principles? I want you to have a personal relationship with God. If you know the God of the Bible, He will enlighten you and give you understanding as you dig into His Word. If you do not know God personally, then I hope this book will challenge you to be open to God.

So let's jump in and find out about the God of the Bible.

Who is God? It is not an easy question to answer because to do so we must use our finite minds to try to grasp the infinite.

Here are some interesting things to consider and attempt to understand with our finite minds.

God is a spirit and has existed forever and is the cause of all things. The Bible does not contain a formal definition of *god*, and it also does not seek to prove His existence formally, as it assumes His existence from the very beginning (Genesis 1:1).

God is not subject to the physical creation, as He resides in the spiritual dimensions of heaven. God created the dimension of time, to which He is not subject.

God is one being in three persons: God the Father, God the Son, and God the Holy Spirit.

God is all-powerful (omnipotent), is all-knowing (omniscient), and is able to be present at all places at all times (omnipresent).

The *Westminster Shorter Catechism* says, "God is spirit, infinite, eternal and unchangeable in his being, his wisdom, his power, his holiness, his justice, his goodness and truth."

Has God been seen? John 1:18 states that no one has seen God at any time. Yet we know that Jesus is the image of the invisible God. We as human beings were created in His image so that God could share His love with us.

God has revealed Himself in science, history, the Bible, and creation itself.

As we close, here is a quick summary: God created the world (Genesis 1:1 and Isaiah 42:5); He actively sustains the world (Colossians 1:17); He is executing His eternal plan (Ephesians 1:11), which involves the redemption of humanity from the curse of sin and death (Galatians 3:13–14); He draws people to Christ (John 6:44); He disciplines His children (Hebrews 12:6); and He will judge the world (Revelation 20:11–15).

God desires that humankind knows Him. Do you know Him? I hope you do.

# 3

## Chapter

# The Bible Is God's Word

As stated prior, these two key principles (the Bible is God's Word and God of the Bible) are of the utmost importance as we jump into eschatology—the study of the end times. I hope you are in acceptance of these two basic principles or are at least open to dig in for yourself and find the truth.

What is the Bible? The Bible consists of sixty-six different books; thirty-nine of these books make up the Old Testament, and twenty-seven books make up the New Testament. There were approximately forty different authors who contributed to the Bible. It was written over a period of about fifteen hundred years. The Bible was written on three different continents and written in three languages: Aramaic, Hebrew, and Greek.

Either the book of Job or the book of Genesis was the first book of the Bible to be written. This was written in approximately 1400 BC. This makes the Bible thirty-four hundred years old today.

The Bible is the most important book in the history of humankind.

There is both internal and external evidence that shows the Bible is truly God's Word.

What is the internal evidence? Here are just four pieces: (1) unity—the Bible is one unified book; (2) the prophecies within the Bible; (3) the unique authority and power of the Bible; and (4) the unique message of the Bible that sets it apart from other religious texts.

What is the external evidence? Here are just three pieces: (1) the historicity of the Bible; (2) the integrity of the human authors; and (3) the indestructibility of the Bible.

History, archaeology, science, and philosophy have shown scripture to be factual and consistent.

The writing of scripture was directed by the Holy Spirit. The Bible does not originate with humanity and is then a product of God and carries the authority of God.

The Bible is infallible, which means incapable of error. The doctrine of infallibility concerns only the original documents.

The Bible is the sole objective source of all God has given us about Himself and His plan for humanity. As God's infallible Word, the Bible is inerrant, authoritative, reliable, and sufficient to meet our needs.

If the Bible is truly the Word of God, then it is the final authority for all matters of faith, religious practice, and morals.

Regular study of the Word of God will give direction and understanding in the issues of life.

The spirit of God, who enlightens us to hear and understand God's Word, takes that knowledge and guides us in living it. The illuminating and leading work of the Holy Spirit in our lives is a confirmation that we are indeed children of God.

Why is the Bible so important in today's world? Most Americans do not believe in moral absolutes. You and I know that the world grows crazier each day. We all must have a set of absolutes to live by—and that is the Bible.

2 Timothy 3:16 reads, "All scripture is God-breathed and is useful for teaching, rebuking, correcting and training in righteousness, so that the man of God may be thoroughly equipped for every good work."

The Bible claims not only to be inspired by God but also to have the supernatural ability to change us and make us complete. I hope that God has made your life complete.

# 4

## Chapter

# Overview of Israel

As we look at the events happening in the world today, most of us get the feeling we are racing toward the end times.

Bad things happen every day—the whole world is in turmoil. Just look at recent attacks in the United States, England, and France. And the United States is involved in a number of wars in the Middle East involving ISIS and their affiliates.

It will continue to get worse over time—guaranteed. And for our kids' and grandkids' sake, may there be some semblance of peace for many years. But God has a plan.

There is only one country and city to focus on as the end times approach. Do not look at New York City, Los Angeles, London, Paris, or Rome. Just keep your eyes on Israel and Jerusalem.

Israel lies in the eye of the storm. Israel and its holy city, Jerusalem, hold the keys to the future.

So let's begin this journey and head to Israel. We will find out what God says throughout the Bible about Israel.

Some general information first. Israel is the size of New Jersey. It consists of 8,630 square miles. It is 290 miles long and 85 miles wide at the widest point.

The population at the end of 2015 was 8.46 million. This includes 6.34 million Jews and 1.76 million Arabs. Experts predict the population of Israel will reach 10 million by 2025 or sooner.

Out of approximately 14.3 million Jewish people in the world today, 43 percent reside in Israel.

What about messianic Jews—those who know Jeshua? It is estimated that there are fifteen thousand messianic Jewish believers in Israel today.

Please refer to the following map, which shows Israel, the surrounding countries, and two areas within Israel.

MEDITERREAN SEA

LEBANON

DAMASCUS

GOLAN HEIGHTS

SYRIA

**ISRAEL AND SURROUNDING COUNTRIES**

WEST BANK

AMMAN

JERUSALEM

DEAD SEA

GAZA

ISRAEL

SINAI

JORDAN

EGYPT

SAUDI ARABIA

RED SEA

Lebanon: Beirut is the capital; almost 5 million population; Muslims are the most numerous; the border with Israel is the blue line established after the 2006 war with Hezbollah in Lebanon; Hezbollah has not disarmed and is even more powerful today.

Syria: Damascus is the capital; almost 23 million population; 90 percent Muslim; civil war ongoing since 2011; President Bashar al-Assad used chemical weapons against his own people in 2013; the United States is involved in the war today against ISIS; Russia is helping the Assad regime; the purple line establishes the border with Israel; Israel occupied the Golan Heights in 1964 and annexed it in 1981; the United Nations observes this boundary.

Jordan: Amman is the capital; population near 10 million; 92 percent Muslim; Jordan captured the West Bank and the old city of Jerusalem during the 1948 Arab-Israeli war; Jordan annexed the West Bank in 1950; Israel took back the West Bank and the old city during the Six-Day War in June 1967; a peace treaty was signed between Jordan and Israel in October 1994.

Egypt: Cairo is the capital; population is 92 million; 90 percent Muslim; Egypt occupied Gaza after the Arab-Israeli war in 1948; during the Six-Day War in 1967, Israel occupied the Sinai Peninsula and the Gaza Strip; a peace treaty was signed between Egypt and Israel in March 1979 in which Israel withdrew from the Sinai and Egypt renounced claims to Gaza; Egypt was the first Arab state to officially recognize Israel.

Gaza: Population is 1.85 million; Egypt seized Gaza in 1948 and then Israel captured Gaza in 1967; Israel granted the Palestinian Authority limited self-government through the Oslo Accords in 1994; in 2005, Israel evacuated Gaza, and today, Gaza is ruled by Hamas.

West Bank: 98 percent Muslim; captured by Jordan in 1948 and included the old city of Jerusalem; Israel took back the West Bank and the old city during the Six-Day War in 1967; today, the Palestinian Authority administers 39 percent of the West Bank, and 61 percent remains under direct Israel military and civilian control; the West Bank makes news often in today's world.

Why show and describe these countries surrounding Israel and the two areas within Israel?

There are 330 million Muslims as neighbors, either on the border or in close proximity, whose primary aim is to annihilate Israel and throw them into the sea.

The 1988 Hamas Charter states that Islam will obliterate Israel.

The West Bank communities today are infiltrated by Hamas and ISIS. One example is the town of Bethlehem. In 1950, Bethlehem and nearby villages were 86 percent Christian; today, it is down to 12 percent.

Regarding the Temple Mount, Israel permits the Waqf, a Muslim nonprofit, to maintain the site and govern its maintenance. Jewish prayers are not allowed on the Temple Mount.

Based on biblical prophecy, there is an upcoming war between Israel and its common border neighbors. This is found in Psalm 83.

Looking beyond the limits of Israel, we find that the United Nations is against Israel. As of 2012, the UN has passed seventy-nine resolutions directly critical of Israel, and 40 percent of the UN Human Rights Council resolutions have been against Israel.

There is worldwide mainstream media bias against Israel, claiming "the illegal occupation of Palestinian lands."

Why is Israel so important?

Did you know that the nation of Israel was created by a sovereign act of God?

Almighty God has already determined the rights of Israel to its land.

The land belongs to God (Leviticus 25:23); God gave the land to the descendants of Abraham (Genesis 12:7); and the land was given because of an unconditional covenant from God, not faithfulness (Genesis 17:7–8).

The old city is the most controversial piece of real estate in the world. Why Jerusalem? Why the Temple Mount? Because that is where Yeshua, Jesus, will return. It is from this area that he will rule in the age to come. His throne will be there.

It is amazing that Israel exists today with nearly the entire world against her. If a person wants a sign from heaven that there is a God and he calls himself the God of Israel, this is it. There is no other rational explanation for Israel's continued existence and success except God.

Israel is the only nation in the world that is governing itself in the same territory, under the same name, and with the same religion and same language as it did three thousand years ago.

My wife and I were in Israel as part of a Holy Land tour in October 2013, and we went back in March 2015. See the following pictures.

U.N. OUTLOOK POST AT
ISRAEL-SYRIAN BORDER

ISRAELI DEFENSE
FORCES (IDF) ON
PRACTICE MANEUVERS IN
GOLAN HEIGHTS

# 5

Chapter

# History and the Future of Israel

The Bible tells us that the nation of Israel was created by a sovereign act of God. God granted or bequeathed the land's title to Israel.

Many nations have attempted to annihilate the Jewish people. For instance, Jerusalem, the City of Peace, has been conquered and reconquered forty-four times.

In AD 135, the Romans dispersed the Jews all across the Roman Empire with the plan that they never come back to the Holy Land.

The Bible prophesies the Jewish people will come back and restore the land (Amos 9:14–15) and there will be a rebirth (Ezekiel 37:21). Please also refer to Isaiah 11:12 and Jeremiah 31:10.

Wake up, world—it has happened. On May 15, 1948, the state of Israel was formed. Yes, you can believe the Bible. The regathering is now well under way, and Israel is taking prominence on the world stage. Again, the Bible prophesies that the God of the Bible will make a name for Himself through Israel in the last days—the world will no longer be able to ignore Him.

What is God's plan? God chose the Jewish people to be His instrument of world redemption. That means that in spite of their sin, God chose them to be the instrument of His revelation and salvation in the world.

Let's go way back in history and note two things. Some twenty-five hundred years before Mohammed was born, Abraham talked with his God, who promised him the Holy Land long before any other current world religion was conceived. And second, the Jewish holy temple stood on Mount Moriah fifteen hundred years before Islamic warriors spread across the Middle East, ultimately conquering great swaths of the earth and forcing Islamic conversion on its citizens.

What about the Promised Land? Let's dig in. The land is described in Genesis 15:18–21 and Numbers 34:1–15.

Please refer to the map later in this chapter.

Israel has not as yet taken the land under the unconditional Abrahamic covenant nor has it ever possessed the whole land.

The Bible has three promises regarding the land.

Promise #1: Abraham, Isaac, and Jacob were promised possession of the land.

Promise #2: The descendants of these three men were promised possession of the land.

Promise #3: Boundaries are listed, but the Jews have never possessed all; therefore, these things must yet come to pass.

How will Israel obtain all of this Promised Land? The Bible prophesies a number of wars that will be occur prior to the Tribulation and be ongoing during the first half of the Tribulation.

Let's mention a few of these wars:

Isaiah 17: Destruction of Damascus, Syria.

Jeremiah 49: Israel and Elam, which is Iran. This could involve the Iran Bushehr nuclear facility.

Ezekiel 29 and 30: This involves the Tower of Syene, the Aswan Dam, and the destruction of Egypt.

Psalm 83: This is a limited war between Israel and its immediate Muslim neighbors.

Ezekiel 38 and 39: This is the Gog and Magog War between Israel and the entire Middle East Muslim countries and Russia.

Let's zero in on the Psalm 83 war, for this is the war in which Israel obtains all of the land that comprises the Holy Land given to Abraham. This war includes the common border nations of Lebanon, Syria, Jordan, Egypt, and the Gaza Strip.

The Israeli IDF forces are victorious in this war. This victory allows Israel to gain great territorial expansion; produces security in Israel; and prosperity is increased and national stature enhanced.

Once Israel realizes all three of these, then the stage is set soon thereafter for the Ezekiel 38–39 Gog and Magog War. This is a war with what is called the outer circle of nations—including Russia, Iran, Ethiopia, Libya, and Turkey. The Bible tells us that God intervenes and all nations against Israel are destroyed.

As stated prior, please know that only God knows the timing and the sequence of these events and wars.

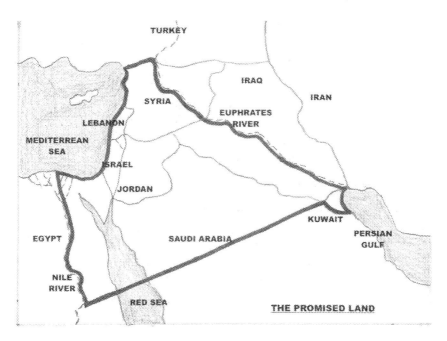

This map is an approximation of what God promised to Abraham. If we apply the boundaries as described in the Bible to the nations today, it would include parts of Egypt, Saudi Arabia, Kuwait, Iraq, and Syria and all of Israel, Lebanon, and Jordan.

# 6

## Chapter

# The World Is Going to Hell

In 2017, Hurricane Harvey hit Texas with a devastating blow. As we watched all the flooding and devastation in and around Houston, we could not comprehend what we were seeing. There was loss of life and loss of houses, cars, and other possessions. Loss of businesses and oil refinery shutdowns affected our whole nation.

We prayed for all the people directly affected by this catastrophic natural disaster. It was obvious that local, state, and federal departments were working overtime to help those involved. It was also good to hear that faith-based organizations played a big role in the recovery efforts.

The reason for mentioning Hurricane Harvey is this: God has a plan for this earth, which includes famines, plagues, horrific weather disruptions, earthquakes, volcano eruptions, one-hundred-pound hailstones, and the earth shifting on breakaway tectonic plates—something this world has never seen before. This is stated in Isaiah 24:1–3, 24:19–21, 30:30 and Revelation 6:14,16:20. This happens during the seven-year Tribulation period.

I don't want you to go through this terrible time—and there is a way for you to escape it. So let's go to the chapter topic: the world is going to hell.

I believe we are getting very close to the end times of this earth as we know it. Each morning as I work in my office or go out on the patio and turn on the news, there is very little good news. Over the last few days, I have heard about the opioid crisis in our country; cars and trucks careening into crowds in Spain and England; more ISIS beheadings; the murder rate in Chicago; M-13 gangs on Long Island; draining the swamp in Washington DC; building a wall; Russian collusion; Black Lives Matter; white supremacists; pulling down statues—it does not end.

Here is my take on all of this: We are witnessing with our own eyes events unfolding that are part of the greatest plan ever for this world. This plan was put into motion some six thousand years ago.

Will we ever see peace on this earth? Sorry to say, the answer is no. And it is only going to get worse. The world is filled with hate. We don't care about life anymore. We slaughter babies. It is not "love thy neighbor"; it is "stab thy neighbor." There is no respect for our law enforcement; we shoot them or won't serve them at restaurants. Now everyone wants medical marijuana, which leads to heroin. Hate groups are flourishing. Pornography is running rampant. It is sex, sex, sex—just take a pill. Why get married? Materialism has taken over. Let's steal from the government; everyone else is. Let's cheat and cut corners; no one will know. LGBT issues. Let's get drunk and have a good time. Let's gamble and lose our families and possessions. Morality is a thing of the past.

What is the greatest plan ever for this earth? It is God's plan. We are all created in God's image. Why are we on this earth? To honor and glorify God and share Him with others.

Satan, a fallen angel, began his influence in the world with Adam and Eve and has been on the loose since. Because of humankind's fall, each of us is born with a sinful nature.

God gave us a free will—we must choose God or Satan during our lifetime. We typically have less than ninety years on this earth until death. And this is but a twinkling of an eye in terms of eternity.

We choose God through His Son, Jesus. Jesus came to die on the cross for our sins.

I plead with you—accept Jesus as Lord and Savior during your lifetime on this earth. Heaven (paradise) and hell (Hades) are real places.

When you die, will your spirit go to be with God in heaven, or will it go to be with Satan forever? Only a few will enter the gates of heaven; will you be one?

God's plan is unfolding. The earth was destroyed by a flood during Noah's time, and now the world will be destroyed by fire.

We see events happening now that are a prelude to Jesus's Second Coming and setting up His kingdom; a new heaven and earth will happen.

The good news is that the church is going to heaven. The church is made up of true born-again believers in Jesus Christ.

You can call yourself a Protestant, a Catholic, a Jew. You can attend a Lutheran, Methodist, Baptist, or Mennonite church; a community church; a Nazarene church; or many other churches. You can even be a member of those churches; that does not count in God's eyes.

What is important is this: God only accepts those who have put their faith in the Lord Jesus Christ and have accepted Jesus as Lord and Savior.

What about America?

We are a post-Christian nation. We have taken God out of everything. We ignore or don't believe the Bible any longer; therefore, there are no absolutes.

Our churches are in a sad state of affairs—only a dim light now. Apostasy in the church is running rampant.

America is not mentioned during the end times. God may allow America to decline to a second-rate country or be destroyed for all of our sins and for ignoring him.

Christians, be forewarned. You will suffer persecution more and more in America. It is already happening.

In the end, God will intervene. Satan will be destroyed.

# 7

## Chapter

# Destruction of Damascus

This chapter deals with the destruction of Damascus. Isaiah 17:1 reads, "See, Damascus will no longer be a city but will become a heap of ruins."

Before we jump in, let me remind you of what Isaiah 46:9–10 says: "Remember the former things, those of long ago; I am God, and there is no other; I am God, and there is none like me. I make known the end from the beginning, from ancient times, what is still to come. I say, my purpose will stand, and I will do all that I please."

Also Isaiah 34:16 reads, "Look in the scroll of the lord and read: none of these will be missing, not one will lack her mate. For it is his mouth that has given the order, and his spirit will gather them together."

God is telling us that all prophecies will come to pass, and we are seeing some of these prophecies come to pass today.

Please refer to the map at the end of this chapter, which shows the close proximity of the Golan Heights to Damascus, Amman, and Jerusalem.

From the border of the Golan Heights with Syria, it is thirty-seven miles to Damascus, eighty-three miles to Amman, and one hundred and forty-nine miles to Jerusalem. This shows you how close these points of interest are in the Isaiah 17 and the Psalm 83 wars.

Regarding the destruction of Damascus, it is just a matter of time before it happens. Isaiah 17:1 reads, "See, Damascus will no longer be a city but will become a heap of ruins." Our eyes are focused on what is happening in Syria today: ISIS has taken a portion of the country; a deadly civil war in ongoing; Russia is there working with President Bashar al-Assad; France, England, and the United States are bombing ISIS targets; Damascus is home to a number of terrorist groups, including Hamas and Hezbollah; and more.

Thousands upon thousands are fleeing Damascus and Syria and looking for safety. Many are refugees in Jordan. And don't forget, Syria has a huge number of chemical weapons stockpiled.

The destruction of Damascus is the next likely event on the prophetic calendar. A provocation will occur in which Israel is attacked, and the IDF retaliates with a nuclear bomb exploding over Damascus, leveling the city in one night. The northern part of Israel will also be destroyed during this war.

In the aftermath of this war, the Psalm 83 war begins with the invasion of Israel from all the surrounding Muslim countries. And yes, God allows Israel to be victorious as He attempts to wake up the Jewish people. More on the Psalm 83 war is forthcoming.

Now some final comments. It is likely that the Isaiah 17 war, which is the destruction of Damascus, will occur just before or during the Psalm 83 war.

Also note that the Bible states these wars will occur "in that day," referring to just before and during the Tribulation period.

How about a little good news? Even though Damascus is destroyed in the Isaiah 17 war, it will exist during the Millennium. Damascus is mentioned a number of times within the boundaries of the "new Holy Land" as given in Ezekiel 47–48.

As a result of these wars, Israel will once again turn to God almighty.

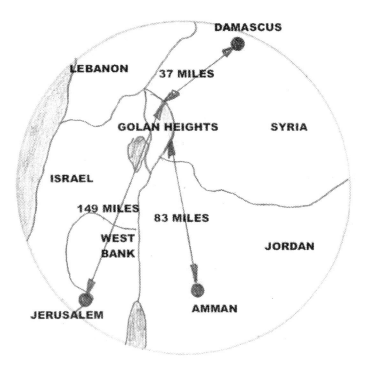

## JERUSALEM, DAMASCUS AND AMMAN

# 8

## Chapter

# Signs of the End Times, Part 1

I thought it would be interesting to look into the signs listed in the Bible that are to occur prior to the Tribulation and see if we are experiencing some of them in today's world. Because of the number of signs to discuss, this will be a two-part series. I will address five more signs in chapter 9.

People are interested in or fascinated with the end times. Even Jesus's own disciples asked about the end times. The Bible states that these end-time signs would be like birth pangs, increasing in frequency and intensity.

Please know that these events are only the beginning of the birth pangs; the end is still to come, but the beginning of the end is here.

We are told in the book of Daniel that many prophecies, events, and signs would not be understood "until the end times." In fact, the Lord told Daniel that at the proper time, "those who are wise will understand" (Daniel 12:10).

We are now able to understand some of these events and signs because our ability to do so depends on past history or technological advances.

The first sign is the nation of Israel, which was recognized in 1948. It was prophesied that Israel would be restored as a political state (Deuteronomy 30:3; Jeremiah 29:14; Amos 9:14–15). We have witnessed this event in our lifetime. My wife and I have had the privilege to visit Israel twice.

The second sign is that people shall be lovers of themselves. Here is one that describes the world we live in today: "People will be lovers of themselves." 2 Timothy 3 warns that in the last days, people shall be lovers of themselves, lovers of money, boastful, proud, abusive, disobedient to their parents, ungrateful, unholy, without love, unforgiving, slanderous, without self-control, brutal, not lovers of good, treacherous, rash, conceited, and lovers of pleasure rather than lovers of God.

Did you catch the last description: lovers of pleasure rather than lovers of God? They will seem godly, but they will deny the power of God through their worldly living. This is the state of the professing Christian world today.

God tells us to turn away from all that was mentioned above.

The third sign is that worldly knowledge and travel will increase. Daniel 12:4 reads, "But you, Daniel, roll up and seal the words of the scroll until the time of the end. Many will go here and there to increase knowledge." There are a couple interpretations of this passage. The first is that we are living in the information and computer age.

We are witnessing huge advances in secular knowledge and technology. It applies to science, medicine, travel, and computers; we see new developments daily.

The second interpretation is there will be great increase in the knowledge of God's truth and prophecies. We have reached a time now in which many people are running to and fro through the scriptures, comparing text to text, and understanding the prophecies. The truth of Bible prophecy has been opened up like never before. With either interpretation, it is evident that this is a sign that we are living in the end times.

The fourth sign is wars and rumors of war. Matthew 24:6–7 reads, "You will hear of wars and rumors of wars, but see to it that you are not alarmed. Such things must happen, but the end is still to come. Nation will rise against nation, and kingdom against kingdom."

War is another sign of the end times. Just turn on the TV; we see wars, violence, and conflicts all over the world. Wars have grown steadily worse since the time of Christ's prophecy.

Let's look at Luke 21:9—it talks about commotions. The definition of *commotion* is disorder, confusion, and tumult. Beyond that, it could include acts and effects of terrorism, such as bombings, but also demonstrations, protests, and riots. Wow; that hits home. We are in the last intermission preceding the greatest war foretold, and that is Armageddon. It only takes the push of a couple buttons to annihilate humankind.

The fifth sign is one world government, currency, and religion. What about one world government? Satan has a plan for a single world government, sometimes referred to as the new world order. We are heading to that end quickly. It is likely that the United Nations will be that entity, with the secretary-general being in command of all nations. The Bible tells about ten toes, and isn't it interesting that the world has already been divided into ten regions? It is probable that Canada, Mexico, and the United States are one of the regions. Do you see some of this happening today?

What about one world currency? As we see in our own time, the world is heading toward one currency. With the use of computers and scanners, we will not have coins and paper money in the future. The Bible tells about all trade and business transactions being made by the use of a chip implanted into our bodies. This is part of Satan's plan and is called the mark of the beast. All this is happening today.

What about one world religion? Satan has a plan for a single humanistic religion for the whole world. Today, we can see this gradually happening. First will come the worship of humankind, and then will come the worship of Satan himself. This likely will be the new Babylon, the revived Roman Empire and the harlot. Look at the apostasy in our churches today. The church age is quickly coming to an end.

# 9

## Chapter

# Signs of the End Times, Part 2

In chapter 8, I discussed five important signs: the nation of Israel; humankind shall be lovers of themselves; worldly knowledge and travel will increase; wars and rumors of war; and one world government, currency, and religion.

In this chapter, I will discuss five more signs.

The sixth sign is false Christs and false prophets. There have always been false teachers, ministers, and prophets in history. The Bible says that during the end times, the number of false teachers, ministers, and prophets will explode; are we seeing this today? Jesus tells us that many, and I say millions, will be deceived—and yes, if possible, even God's elect.

Who should we look out for: healing movements, prosperity gospel movements, people like David Koresh and Jim Jones, satanic cults, spiritualist cults, new age cults, Bible-believing cults, and many more. How do you overcome this? Study the greatest book ever (the Bible), hold on to the truths therein, and focus on Jesus's return to earth.

In 1 Timothy 4:1, "the spirit clearly says that in later times some will abandon the faith and follow deceiving spirits and things taught by demons."

Matthew 24:4–5 says to "watch out that no one deceives you. For many will come in my name, claiming, I am the messiah, and will deceive many."

Matthew 24:24 says, "For false messiahs and false prophets will appear and perform great signs and wonders to deceive, if possible, even the elect."

The seventh sign is the increase in persecution, which will lead to many martyrs. Christians, beware—it will only get worse, and you will be subject to increasing tribulation, trials, troubles, afflictions, and persecution. Not during my lifetime and I hope for many years to come, but our children and grandchildren could face extreme persecution in the form of imprisonment, beatings, torture, and loss of life.

The Bible is very clear regarding persecution:

2 Timothy 3:12: "In fact, everyone who wants to live a godly life in Christ Jesus will be persecuted."

John 15:18: "If the world hates you, keep in mind that it hated me first."

Matthew 5:10–12: "Blessed are those who are persecuted because of righteousness, for theirs is the kingdom of heaven. Blessed are you when people insult you, persecute you, and falsely say all kinds of evil against you because of me. Rejoice and be glad, because great is your reward in heaven, for in the same way they persecuted the prophets who came before you."

How will you face persecution? Will you face it with fear or with faith? Everyone who publicly lives a committed Christian life will face some kind of resistance from the world. Casual Christians (those who only play the game and are loved by the world) know nothing about spiritual warfare. In fact, the Bible tells us that as persecution increased, "the love of most will grow cold" (Matthew 24:12). Also many professing Christians will "turn away" from the faith and will betray and hate one another (Matthew 24:10). The same thing is indicated in 2 Timothy 3:2–3, which says that people will "not be lovers of good," and therefore they will be "brutal" and "ungrateful," reviling those who stand for righteousness.

The eighth sign includes famine, pestilences, and earthquakes.

Please refer to Matthew 24:7; Mark 13:8; and Luke 21:11.

Jesus said, "There will be famines." Famines are increasing now, and in the future, there will be extreme worldwide famine. Over nine million people die each year from hunger and hunger related diseases.

(theworldcounts.com and mercycorps.org).

Jesus said, "There shall be pestilences," which also means diseases. Disease will soon alter the course of history; the diseases that this world suffers from are a sign that we are in the last days. Our food sources are also being contaminated more and more. You think we have terrible epidemics now; just wait for the upcoming worldwide pandemics. The death toll from disease is approximately thirty million per year and growing.

Jesus said, "There shall be earthquakes in various places." An earthquake expert has that said the earth is cracking up. Jesus tells us that earthquakes will increase in frequency and intensity during the end times. Current graphs clearly show an alarming worldwide trend of increasing earthquake strength and frequency. These results are in agreement with the USGS statistics.

The ninth sign is "the gospel will be preached to the whole world." Matthew 24:14 reads, "And the gospel of the kingdom will be preached in the whole world as a testimony to all nations, and then the end will come." Did you hear that? Once the true gospel message is preached to the whole world—aren't we getting close to that? We are using television, books, radio, missions, and the internet to share this message around the world today. Once God determines that all have heard, the church age will come to an end. We are definitely in the end times.

The tenth sign is the rapture. This is more than a sign—it is an event! It will be a sign to those who remain after the rapture. Now that I have shared this, you know that I am of the persuasion that the rapture takes place prior to the Tribulation—thus pre-trib. In all fairness, there are those who believe the rapture occurs at the middle of the Tribulation—mid-trib; at the end of the Tribulation—post-trib; and those who hold the pre-wrath position. If you wish, please study these four positions on the timing of the rapture.

I will proceed based on the pre-trib position. 1 Thessalonians 4:16–17 reads, "For the lord himself will come down from heaven, with a loud command, with the voice of the archangel and with the trumpet call of God, and the dead in Christ will rise first. After that, we who are still alive and are left will be caught up together with them in the clouds to meet the lord in the air. And so we will be with the lord forever." Here we see the Lord appears in the heavens and supernaturally draws the church, living and dead, to Him.

1 Thessalonians 1:10 tells why this happens: "and to wait for his son from heaven, whom he raised from the dead—Jesus, who rescues us from the coming wrath." Thus all believers will be in heaven during the seven-year Tribulation. At the end of the Tribulation, the armies in heaven (the church) follow Christ as He returns to earth. The armies ride on white horses, clothed in fine linen, white and clean. How exciting will that be!

When does the rapture occur in relation to the beginning of the Tribulation? There is a gap between these two events that will last a few years—possibly three to five years. The Tribulation is kicked off by the signing of a peace treaty between Israel and its surrounding Arab countries.

I pray that you are prepared for the imminent return of the Lord to receive His church—the rapture of the saints.

I have mentioned and discussed ten signs of the end times. These are major signs, but know there are other signs happening today that indicate we are in the end times. The end is still to come.

Make sure you are prepared for the end time. 2 Corinthians 6:2 states, "In the time of my favor I heard you, and in the day of salvation I helped you, I tell you, now is the time of God's favor, now is the day of salvation."

# 10

## Chapter

# Jesus Born in September

Jesus—Yeshua—was born in late September. Yes, you read that right. Jesus was born in late September—not December 25, as we celebrate today.

How do we know this? The Bible tells us. If you dig in and study Luke 1 and 2, you will find that John the Baptist was born during Passover in 5 BC. Jesus was born six months later during the Festival of Tabernacles in 5 BC, which is the month of September.

Here are some particulars:

Who was at Jesus's birth? Joseph, Mary, the baby Jesus, and angels, and then the shepherds came just after the birth.

Jesus was circumcised on the eighth day. Then on the fortieth day, Joseph, Mary, and Jesus traveled to Jerusalem to consecrate Jesus and offer a sacrifice of two doves. While in Jerusalem, Simeon and Anna prophesied over Jesus, declaring him to be the Messiah and Redeemer.

Finally, let's talk about the magi, also known as the wise men, from Matthew 2:1. Did you know that Jesus was fifteen months old when the wise men came to Bethlehem? They came in their official role to confer upon Jesus the title of king and high priest of Israel. This likely happened at the Jewish festival of Hanukkah or Feast of Dedication.

It is interesting to note that the magi would have come around the time we now celebrate Christmas, December 25.

The date of December 25 was first observed in AD 336. Pope Julius I chose to replace a pagan winter feast with what has become Christmas. The holiday was officially recognized in the United States in 1870.

Was Jesus's birth prophesied in the Old Testament? There are over three hundred prophecies about the coming Messiah. Yeshua, which means "salvation" or "God saves," is mentioned over 150 times in the Old Testament.

Micah 5:2 prophesies Christ's birth seven hundred years before His birth.

The clearest prophecy of Jesus is found in Isaiah 53.

Verses 5 to 7: "But he was pierced for our transgressions, he was crushed for our iniquities, the punishment that brought us peace was on him, and by his wounds we are healed. We all, like sheep, have gone astray, each of us has turned to our own way, and the lord has laid on him the iniquity of us all. He was oppressed and afflicted, yet he did not open his mouth, he was led like a lamb to the slaughter, and as a sheep before its shearers is silent, so he did not open his mouth."

I am not here to argue the birth date of our Lord and Savior. I am thankful we celebrate on December 25 and give gifts just as the magi did. In the giving of gifts, may we never forget the greatest gift ever.

God became a human being in order to bring salvation to the whole world.

And now, over two thousand years later, we look for Christ's return. Are you ready to meet Him? I hope you are.

# 11
## Chapter

# Humankind's Timeline on Earth

First, let's discuss God's creation of you and me. God created us in His own image (Genesis 1:27).

And yes—time. God divided the light from the darkness. God called the light day and the darkness night, and the evening and the morning were the first day (Genesis 1:5).

And yes—space. God created the heaven and the earth (Genesis 1:1) and the sun, moon, and stars (Genesis 1:14).

So God created humankind within the confines of time and space. Time is the measurement of life (James 4:14). Time is also the measurement of decay. So the timeline of a person's life on this earth reflects various stages of maturity and decay.

In terms of space, we live in the first heaven, which is our immediate atmosphere. Humankind also travels into the second heaven, which is where the sun, moon, and stars are located. The third heaven is the home of God (Hebrews 8:1, 9:24).

God is spirit. He exists outside the bounds of time, space, and matter. Revelation 10:6 states, "There will be no more delay."

Please refer to the sketch at the end of this chapter.

We live on earth and within the first heaven. Humankind has traveled into the second heaven via space travel and has landed on the moon. So we live in the confines of time and space. God is spirit and lives in the third heaven—the realm of eternity. God lives outside the bounds of time, space, and matter.

When we die on this earth, our spirits will either go to the realm of heaven or the realm of hell.

So let's zero in on our topic. I wish to establish a possible time for this earth since God's creation week and ending at the end of the thousand-year Millennium. The reason for this is to place on that timeline where we are in the year 2018.

I do not have definitive answers, but I can share some timeline possibilities from a number of Bible scholars, Jewish rabbis, the Bible, and other sources:

1.  Jewish feasts: The seven feasts given to Israel as appointed times are also prophetical. Colossians 2:17 says these are "a shadow of things to come." The first four feasts: Passover, unleavened bread; Pentecost, and firstfruits take us from spring to harvest and have been fulfilled. The three fall feasts remind that winter is ahead and are unfulfilled. These include trumpets, atonement, and tabernacles. The Torah has several instructions relating to groups

of six days or years followed by a seventh that is unique. God has revealed His seven-thousand-year plan for humanity.

2. Dispensations: Dispensations are a humanmade way of understanding God's work. There are seven dispensations: innocence, conscience, human government, promise, law, grace, and the Millennial kingdom of Christ. We now live in the grace period.

3. Archbishop James Ussher (1581–1656), ordained priest in the Anglican church, assumed the Bible to be the only reliable source of chronological information for the time periods covered therein. He wrote *The Annals of the World* and published it in 1650. His study puts the creation at 4004 BC, so add 2,018 years to this, and it adds up the 6,022 years.

4. Seven-day creation week: 2 Peter 3:8 says, "With the lord a day is like a thousand years, and a thousand years are like a day." This leads to six thousand years of humankind's rule and then one thousand years of Jesus's rule on this earth.

5. Ancient book of Enoch: The first- and second-century church fathers quoted this book and believed it contained genuine prophecy. The book was not added to the canon of scripture but was highly respected. This includes a ten-week prophecy with each week representing seven hundred years. The tenth week ends at AD 3075 with the Millennium beginning at AD 2075. This means that Christ's Second Coming could occur in 2075 or sooner.

6. School of Elijah: Listed are three distinct periods of time: age of chaos, age of Torah (law), and the days of Messiah. Each period is to last two thousand years. The church age began in either AD 32 or AD 70, thus ending in AD 2032 or AD 2070.

7. Ancient church fathers and the epistle of Barnabas: All of the following promoted seven thousand years of history: Irenaeus, Hippolytus, Victorinus, Methodius, Lactantius, and the epistle of Barnabus 15:7–9.

8. Seven churches of Revelation 2–3: Some biblical scholars believe that God is foreshadowing the seven stages of the gospel church

and seven different periods in the history of the church. We are now living in the apostate church age of Laodicea, which is from the year 1900 until the Tribulation.

I have found another source that claims Christ could return as early as 2030 if the Sabbath years 2024–2030 coincide with the seventieth week of Daniel. Another source indicates the year 2110, which allows for 110 years maximum for Adam and Eve in the garden.

There are many other sources you can search if you wish to dig in.

What does the Bible say about our time on this earth?

James 4:14: "Why, you do not even know what will happen tomorrow. What is your life? You are a mist that appears for a little while and then vanishes."

Job 14:2: "They spring up like flowers and wither away; like fleeting shadows, they do not endure."

Psalm 39:4–6: "Show me lord, my life's end and the number of my days, let me know how fleeting my life is. You have made my days a mere handbreadth, the span of my years is as nothing before you. Everyone is but a breath, even those who seem secure. Surely everyone goes around like a mere phantom, in vain they rush about, heaping up wealth without knowing whose it will finally be."

From these verses we see that in God's sight, our lives on this earth are like vapor, shadows, fleeting, and the span of our lives are as nothing compared to eternity.

Please refer to the charts at the end of this chapter.

The first chart shows seven thousand years from creation to the end of the Millennium.

The upper numbers and dates indicate the Jewish timeline based on ancient church fathers, feasts, and the school of Elijah. Here we have three sets of two thousand years plus the Millennium.

The lower numbers and dates indicate the book of Enoch timeline. Here we have ten sets of seven hundred years adding up to seven thousand years, which ends in the year 7000 AM or AD 3075. "AM" is called Anno Mundi for the year after creation.

On this timeline, we show when Enoch was born, Noah's flood, Solomon's temple destroyed, and Jesus's ascension. The connection between these timelines occurs with Solomon's temple being destroyed in 3388 AM, which is 587 BC.

The second chart shows the timeline from 1970 to 2110. Here are the time ranges we have mentioned:

Second Coming 1975–2075

Church age ends 2032–2070, the years 2030 and 2110

And below I have two lines—each showing a typical eighty-year human lifespan. The first line is for someone forty years old today—ending 2059. The other is for a newborn today—ending 2099.

Why am I sharing this timeline? I am not setting dates or trying to be sensational but only sharing what others before have presented. Time could be very short. My heart's desire is for you to know God through His Son, Jesus, and accept Him during your lifetime on this earth.

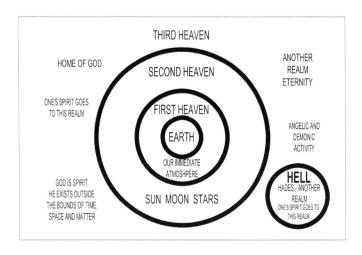

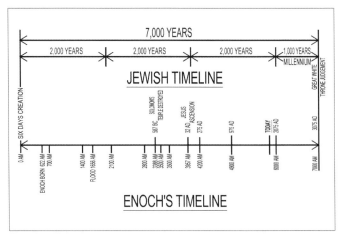

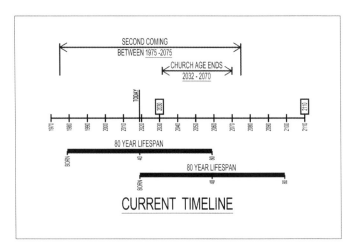

# 12

## Chapter

# Glorified Bodies

So you have heard the old saying that two things are for certain in life: taxes and death. Let's forget taxes for now and talk about death. What happens to you at death? We are going to find out what the Bible says.

In chapter 11, we learned about humankind's time on this earth. We read James 4:14, Job 14:2, and Psalm 39:4–6. From these verses, we see that in God's sight, our lives on this earth are fleeting.

Humankind was created as a triune being—body, soul, and spirit. For this discussion, I will combine the soul and spirit as one in the same. So each of us has a spirit and this spirit never dies. At our death, the spirit is separated from the body.

You may ask—is there life after death? And where do I go when I die?

Let's answer the first question. John 3:16: "For God so loved the world that he gave his one and only son, that whoever believes in him shall not perish but have eternal life"; 1 Corinthians 2:9: "What no eye has seen, what no ear has heard, and what no human mind has conceived—the things God has prepared for those who love him"; and John 11:25–26: "I am the resurrection and the life. The one who believes in me will live, even though they die; and whoever lives by believing in me will never die."

Now to the second question—where do I go when I die? Only you can determine where you go when you die. And there are only two options: either heaven or hell.

Please refer to the chart at the end of this chapter.

When Christians die—those who have truly accepted Jesus as Lord and Savior—their fully conscious spirits are ushered immediately into the presence of Jesus. 2 Corinthians 5:8 reads, "We are confident, I say, and would prefer to be away from the body and at home with the lord." Luke 23:43 reads, "Jesus answered him, truly I tell you, today you will be with me in paradise." 2 Corinthians 12:4 reads, "I was caught up to paradise."

Non-Christians' spirits are immediately taken to Hades, commonly known as hell—a place of conscious suffering and despair, a place of torment. Revelation 1:18 reads, "I am the living one, I was dead, and now look, I am alive forever and ever, and I hold the keys of death and Hades"; Revelation 20:13 also refers to death and Hades.

We have been talking about our spirits up till now; let's discuss what happens to our bodies.

In today's world, once a person dies, his or her body is buried in a casket and vault, or increasingly the body is cremated and the ashes put in an urn.

Believers will receive our glorified and resurrected bodies when the Lord returns for his church. 1 Thessalonians 4:16–17 reads, "For the lord himself will come down from heaven, with a loud command, with the voice of the archangel and with the trumpet call of God, and the dead in Christ will rise first. After that we who are still alive and are left will be caught up together with them in the clouds to meet the lord in the air. And so we will be with the lord forever."

What a wonderful picture: Jesus brings our spirits with Him, resurrects our bodies, reunites our spirits with our bodies, and glorifies our bodies.

We will reign on this earth for a thousand years, called the Millennium, and then be judged at the great white throne judgment. Please refer to Revelation 20:11–15. Believers will be judged by Christ, and we will be rewarded, not punished according to our deeds. After we receive our rewards, we will enter the new heaven and the new earth.

Nonbelievers' bodies remain in the grave during the thousand-year Millennium. At the end of the Millennium, their bodies are resurrected with their spirits and taken to the great white throne judgment. Those who names are not in the book of life are thrown into the eternal lake of fire.

Let's end this discussion with a few thoughts about our glorified bodies.

We will be recognizable in our glorified bodies (Matthew 17:3–4); we will be clothed in white garments, pure, undefiled by sin (Revelation 3:4–5, 18). How about these attributes: imperishable bodies; no sickness or death; not subject to heat, cold, hunger, thirst; empowered by the Holy Spirit; have form and solidity to touch; no hindrance to travel; and enjoy food.

We will be made of flesh and bone—no blood. Our new bodies will be made of a framework of bones suitable for a spirit body. Our flesh, not human flesh, will be adapted to the spirit world.

Our present faculties and powers will be wonderfully multiplied. And think about this: we will pass with the swiftness of lightning from earth to heaven and back.

I want you to live eternally with Jesus. Do you know Him personally? You control your future: heaven or hell. Please accept Jesus as your Lord and Savior.

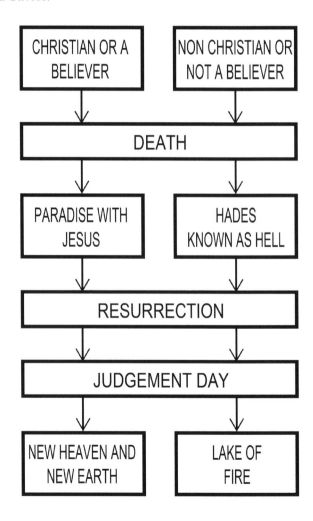

# 13

## Chapter

# Twelve Tribes of Israel

This chapter deals with the twelve tribes of Israel. You may ask what this has to do with future events and the end times.

But first let's go back in history to 1730 BC. That is when Joseph was sold by his brothers for twenty pieces of silver. I want to start here and end in approximately 1400 BC, when the Promised Land was divided among the twelve tribes of Israel (Joshua 13:8–17:18).

Let's hit some highlights during this time frame. Joseph was sold to the Midianites, who then took Joseph to Egypt, where he was sold to a man named Potiphar, a king's official (Genesis 37).

Joseph rose in power and became the viceroy of Egypt, appointed by the pharaoh. Joseph tells the pharaoh that seven years of famine will soon come, so Egypt takes seven years to prepare for the famine. The famine affects the land of Canaan, and Jacob takes his family of seventy to Egypt, where they become slaves. During the next 430 years, the Israelites prosper and multiply to about three million people (Exodus 1:19).

Moses then asks the pharaoh if he could lead his people out of Egypt and is told no. So the ten plagues hit Egypt, and Moses leads the Israelites across the Red Sea to Mount Sinai.

God gives Moses the Ten Commandments at this time, which the Israelites are to follow. Due to their disobedience, they wander in the desert for forty years. They finally reach the Promised Land, but Moses dies prior to entering.

Joshua leads the people into the Promised Land in 1405 BC. Seven years later, in 1398, the land of Canaan is divided among the children of Israel (Joshua 14).

Here are the twelve tribes, all sons and grandsons of Jacob: Asher, Benjamin, Dan, Ephraim, Gad, Isaachar, Judah, Manasseh, Naphtali, Reuben, Simeon, and Zebulon.

Please refer to the map at the end of this chapter.

After King Solomon died in 930 BC, ten of the tribes formed the independent kingdom of Israel in the north and the other two tribes (Judah and Benjamin) set up the kingdom of Judah in the south.

What happened to the northern kingdom of Israel? The ten tribes were defeated in a war with the Neo-Assyrian empire and deported in 722 BC (it lasted 208 years).

What happened to the southern kingdom of Judah? The two tribes were defeated by the Babylonians and were exiled to Babylon in 597 BC (it lasted 334 years). The Jewish temple was destroyed in 586 BC.

So where are the twelve tribes today? There are volumes of books and articles out there explaining where the tribes are, in the United

States, England, and most countries of the world. But the truth is, the tribes were never lost. God knows where they are.

By the way, do you know which tribe Jesus came from? Jesus is a member of the tribe of Judah by lineage (Matthew 1:1–6; Luke 3:31–34). Revelation 5:5 states that Jesus is the lion of the tribe of Judah.

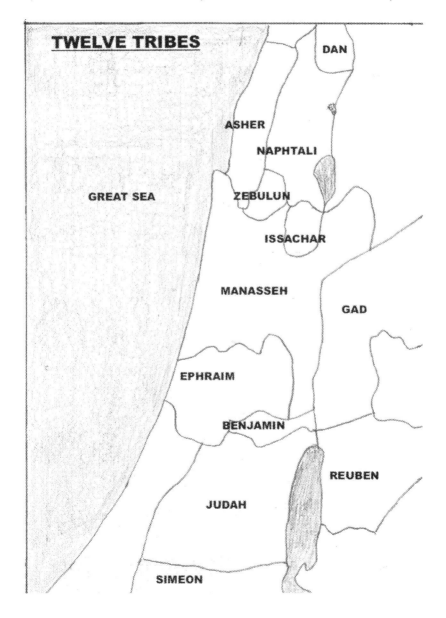

# 14
## Chapter

# 144,000

In chapter 13, we learned that Joshua led the Israelites to the Promised Land in 1451 BC. Thirteen tribes actually left Egypt—they are Asher, Benjamin, Dan, Ephraim, Gad, Issachar, Judah, Manasseh, Naphtali, Reuben, Simeon, Zebulon, and the Levites.

Twelve tribes were given land; the tribe of Levi became the priesthood of the Israelites and were not given land.

We then learned the ten northern tribes and the two southern tribes were defeated in 722 BC and 597 BC, respectively. Some were killed, some dispersed to countries far away, and some came back to the area.

Volumes have been written as to their whereabouts. One thing is for certain: the tribes were never lost. God knows where they are.

James 1:1 reads, "To the twelve tribes scattered among the nations." The twelve tribes of Israel are still in existence and will be in the messianic kingdom.

Please go to Revelation 7:1–8 and see the tribes listed. Reading carefully, we see that Dan is missing and also that Levi is included. The Bible does not tell us why Dan is omitted. Common speculation is because of their idolatry—Dan was the first tribe to commit this type of grievous sin.

So why are the 144,000 so important? Let's jump ahead to the upcoming seven-year Tribulation period. This period of time is spelled out in Daniel 9:24–27. Why have a Tribulation period? This is the time God will enact divine judgment against those who reject Him and will complete His plan of salvation for the nation of Israel.

The Tribulation begins when the Antichrist signs a peace accord with Israel. The world follows the Antichrist during the Tribulation— we can see the beginnings of this today as we head to one world government, one world currency, and one world religion.

Why does the Antichrist have so much success? It is because those who know Jesus personally have been removed from this earth in the rapture. The rapture occurs a short time prior to the Tribulation.

So let's talk about the role of the 144,000 during the Tribulation.

God will place an angelic seal on the 144,000—making them His possession. This will give them a special protection of God from all divine judgments and from the Antichrist.

Revelation 7:3 states they will teach the truth to the whole world.

As a result of their ministry, "a great multitude that no one could count, from every nation, tribe, people and language will come to faith in Christ" (Revelation 7:9).

But know this—most if not all of this multitude of Gentiles and the 144,000 Jews will be slain and martyred during the seven-year Tribulation period.

It is my hope that you know Jesus personally and will be taken up to meet Jesus at the rapture. I do not want you to endure the most horrendous times and likely be killed during the Tribulation.

# 15

## Chapter

# Today's World

Chapter 15 begins a four-part series that takes us from today all the way to the Millennium and the new heaven and new earth. We begin our study with what I call "today's world." The world is now in the church age—sometimes called the times of the Gentiles. Chapter 15 begins with 1948 and goes to the rapture.

Why 1948? This is a very important date in history—the state of Israel was recognized as a sovereign country. God says in Amos 9:14–15, "And I will bring my people Israel back from exile. They will rebuild the ruined cities and live in them. They will plant vineyards and drink their wine, they will make gardens and eat their fruit. I will plant Israel in their own land, never again to be uprooted from the land I have given them, says the lord your God."

This is amazing. God said it would happen, and it happened in my lifetime. Millions of Jewish people are returning to Israel, to the land that God promised them.

We end this discussion at the rapture; this is the catching away of believers that make up the true church. The rapture is imminent; that means it could happen at any moment. It is the next event on the prophetic calendar; there are no other events that must happen prior to the rapture.

I will be presenting the pre-trib rapture in this series. Here are some key verses that shows the church is not appointed to the wrath of God.

Romans 5:9: "Since we have now been justified by his blood, how much more shall we be saved from God's wrath through him."

1 Thessalonians 1:10: "And to wait for his son from heaven, whom he raised from the dead—Jesus, who rescues us from the coming wrath."

1 Thessalonians 5:9: "For God did not appoint us to suffer wrath but to receive salvation through our lord Jesus Christ."

Here are some key verses for the rapture.

1 Thessalonians 4:16–18: "For the lord himself will come down from heaven, with a loud command, with the voice of the archangel and with the trumpet call of God, and the dead in Christ will rise first. After that, we who are still alive and are left will be caught up together with them in the clouds to meet the lord in the air. And so we will be with the lord forever. Therefore encourage one another with these words."

1 Corinthians 15:51–52: "Listen, I tell you a mystery, we will not all sleep, but we will all be changed. In a flash, in the twinkling of an eye, at the last trumpet. For the trumpet will sound, the dead will be raised imperishable, and we will be changed."

What are we going to see and experience in this world as we get closer to the rapture and seven-year Tribulation?

It is apparent that the world is moving further away from biblical principles. Here in the United States, we have kicked God out of almost everything, including some churches. Because of this there are no absolutes; humankind has made themselves God.

A big key is to watch our world head to one world government, one currency, and one religion. We see this happening on a regular basis.

The following verses hit it on the head. 2 Timothy 3:1–5 states, "There will be terrible times in the last days. People will be lovers of themselves, lovers of money, boastful, proud, abusive, disobedient to their parents, ungrateful, unholy, without love, unforgiving, slanderous, without self control, brutal, not lovers of good, treacherous, rash, conceited, lovers of pleasure rather than lovers of God."

1 Timothy 4:1 and Matthew 24:4–5 state that there will be an increase in false Christs and false prophets.

2 Timothy 3:12 and Matthew 5:10–12 state that there will be an increase in persecution.

Guess what? This is God's plan; it is spelled out in the Bible. Please dig in for yourself and check out God's plan. He wants you to know His Son, Jesus, personally.

Don't forget Revelation 1:3: "Blessed is the one who reads aloud the words of this prophecy, and blessed are those who hear it and take to heart what is written in it, because the time is near."

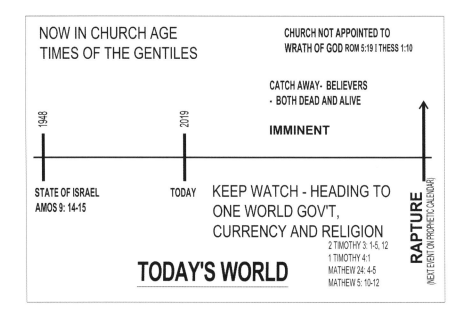

NOW IN CHURCH AGE
TIMES OF THE GENTILES

CHURCH NOT APPOINTED TO
WRATH OF GOD ROM 5:19 I THESS 1:10

CATCH AWAY- BELIEVERS
- BOTH DEAD AND ALIVE

1948

2019

**IMMINENT**

STATE OF ISRAEL
AMOS 9: 14-15

TODAY

KEEP WATCH - HEADING TO
ONE WORLD GOV'T,
CURRENCY AND RELIGION
2 TIMOTHY 3: 1-5, 12
1 TIMOTHY 4:1
MATHEW 24: 4-5
MATHEW 5: 10-12

**TODAY'S WORLD**

RAPTURE
(NEXT EVENT ON PROPHETIC CALENDAR)

# 16

# Gap Period

You may ask—why a gap period?

Many events must happen after the rapture and prior to signing a covenant, which begins the seven-year Tribulation. Let's discuss some highlights.

When the rapture occurs, all the dead in Christ will rise to meet the Lord, then we who are alive and born again will be transformed and meet the Lord in midair.

All Christians will then be judged in heaven at the Bema Seat of Christ. Jesus will hand out five heavenly crowns based on works that we did after receiving Christ as Lord and Savior. These crowns are the imperishable crown, crown of rejoicing, crown of righteousness, crown of glory, and crown of life.

This is the time that the Holy Spirit as a restrainer is removed. Why? Because the Holy Spirit lives within the hearts and souls of all believers.

Can you imagine what happens on this earth and to the many who remain? There will be complete turmoil, lawlessness, and civil disobedience. There will be deep distress in the masses left behind because many will lose their loved ones.

It will take time for this global turmoil to settle down. Jesus opens the first of seven seals at this time (Revelation 6:1), and the Antichrist is revealed by a white horse.

The revived Roman Empire (Daniel 7:23–25), which is the fourth world kingdom, rises and develops strength. The global false religion led by the great harlot dominates (Revelation 17). All of this takes time during the gap period, and some say this could last up to ten years.

Jesus will be opening more seals during this time: seal #2 (Revelation 6:3), which reveals a red horse indicating wars, and seal #3 (Revelation 6:5), which reveals a black horse indicating famine.

Please note the wars likely to occur during the gap period: Isaiah 17, Jeremiah 49, Psalm 83, and the Ezekiel 38–39 Gog and Magog War.

Another event is the building of the Jewish temple (2 Thessalonians 2:4). This will take time to construct and be used by the Jews, including sacrifices. The temple must be functioning prior to the middle of the Tribulation, when the Antichrist moves into the temple.

We are told in the Ezekiel 38–39 war that Israel will be forced out of the land at the middle of the Tribulation (Matthew 24:16). It states that it will take seven years to burn all the debris from the war and bury the dead. Working backward, this means that this period of time occurs three and a half years into the gap period.

One final event to discuss and found in 1 Thessalonians 5:3 is a time of peace required for the Daniel 9:27 covenant to be signed. Israel is a party to this covenant along with the Antichrist and an overflowing scourge found in Isaiah 28:15 known as "Death and Sheol."

Once this covenant is signed, the seven-year Tribulation officially begins.

As Christians, why should we care? Whether it is a spouse, child, grandchild, friend, neighbor, coworker, or someone else in our spheres of influence, we want them to accept Christ prior to the rapture. Otherwise, they have a very high risk of being killed for their faith during the Tribulation. If they never accept Christ, they will be eternally damned and placed in hell.

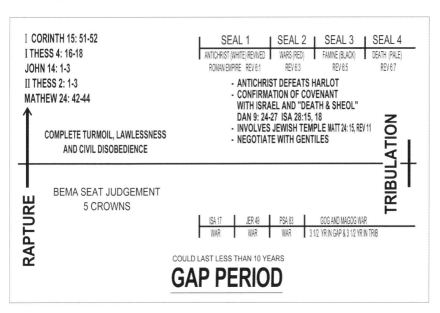

## 17

Chapter

# The Tribulation

Are you ready to learn about the Tribulation? This is a seven-year period of time the likes of which our world has never seen. There will be complete devastation, and billions of people will die. This is the time that God takes His eyes off of the church and focuses on Israel.

The signing and confirmation of a covenant between the Antichrist, Israel, and "Death and Sheol" starts the Tribulation. After seven years, the Tribulation comes to an end with the Battle of Armageddon and the Second Coming of Christ (Revelation 19:7–21).

I want to interject at this point—I personally believe in a pre-trib rapture. All born-again believers, both dead and alive, will meet Jesus in midair prior to the seven-year Tribulation. I want to mention three other positions on when the rapture occurs: there are mid-tribbers, who believe the rapture occurs at the three-and-a-half-year mark; there are the post-tribbers, who believe the rapture occurs at the end of the Tribulation; and there are the pre-wrath tribbers, who believe the rapture occurs when seal #7 is opened. I believe the Bible clearly states that we, as the church, will not go through any of the seven-year Tribulation.

Now let's look at just a few important events that happen during these seven years.

Jesus continues to open the seals; I believe that at least three seals are opened during the gap period. The remaining seals are opened during the Tribulation. The seventh seal opens the seven trumpets, and the seventh trumpet opens the seven bowls.

The seven seals are found in Revelation 6:1–17.

The seven trumpets are found in Revelation 8:1–9:21.

The seven bowls are found in Revelation 16:1–21.

The lists of the seals, trumpets, and bowls are located at the end of this chapter.

You do not want to be part of any of this; please accept Jesus now as your Savior.

I need to mention the seven thunders found in Revelation 10:1–7. John, who wrote the book of Revelation, was told to seal up what the seven thunders have said and do not write it down. These are the only words in Revelation that are sealed. This happens between the sixth and seventh trumpets. It is likely that this judgment was simply too terrifying to be recorded.

There will be two witnesses who prophesy for 1,260 days, which is the first half of the Tribulation. These will be two humans who have the spirit and power of Moses and Elijah. The Antichrist kills both of these men, and after three and a half days, they are miraculously raised from the dead (Revelation 11:3–12).

After the rapture and during the Tribulation, 144,000 Jews will be sealed by God; they will preach and teach, and multitudes will be saved (Revelation 7:3–9).

Midway through the Tribulation, the abomination of desolation takes place. This is when the Antichrist enters the Jewish temple and declares himself to be God. The Antichrist will make some kind of image that all are forced to worship (Daniel 9:27; Revelation 13:14).

The Tribulation ends with the Battle of Armageddon; the Antichrist, the false prophet, and Satan will inspire the armies of the world to invade Israel, kill all the Jews, and fight against Christ. This battle encompasses most of Israel but is centered in the valley of Megiddo. Jesus returns to earth along with his army and defeats the Antichrist (Revelation 16:12–16, 19:7–21).

I want you to be part of the winning team; accept Jesus now.

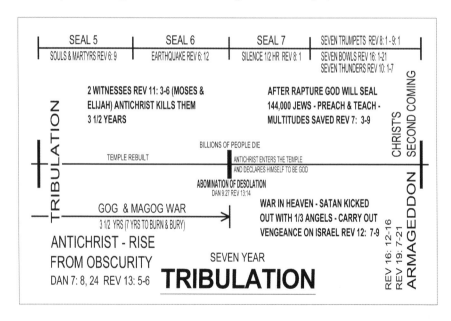

# Seven Seals
## Revelation 6:1–17

First Seal: White horse—introduces the Antichrist

Second Seal: Red horse—great warfare

Third Seal: Black horse—famine

Fourth Seal: Pale horse—death

Fifth Seal: Scene in heaven—souls, host of martyrs

Sixth Seal: Great worldwide earthquake

Seventh Seal: God calls for silence for a half-hour. Last chance to obtain mercy. Opens seven trumpets.

# Seven Trumpets
## Revelation 8:1–9:21

First Trumpet: Worldwide hailstorm with fire

Second Trumpet: Fiery mountain crashes—meteor

Third Trumpet: Wormwood—meteor

Fourth Trumpet: Sun and moon darkened—one-third light

Fifth Trumpet: Hell opened for five months—scorpions

Sixth Trumpet: Release four demonic angels—armies

Seventh Trumpet: Calls forth seven angels with seven bowls of wrath

The fifth, sixth, and seventh trumpets are known as the three woes of Revelation.

## Seven Bowls
Revelation 16:1–21

First Bowl: Boils, painful sores

Second Bowl: Sea life dead

Third Bowl: Rivers turn to blood

Fourth Bowl: Sun's heat

Fifth Bowl: Great darkness

Sixth Bowl: Euphrates dried up—armies, Armageddon

Seventh Bowl: Earthquake, hailstones, loud voice from throne "It is done."

Tribulation closing.

## Rapture
1 Thessalonians 4:13–18 means "catching away."

Four main views:

1. Pre-trib: believers caught up to be with Christ before the Tribulation begins.
2. Mid-trib: believers taken in the middle of Tribulation.
3. Pre-wrath: believers caught up in second half of Tribulation, between sixth and seventh seals.
4. Post-trib: believers raptured at end of Tribulation when Christ returns.

# 18

## Chapter

# The Millennium

We now come to the Millennium: a thousand-year time when Jesus reigns on this earth.

As I mentioned before, there is so much that happens during the Tribulation and now the Millennium that I can only share some highlights; I hope this sparks an interest in you and that you will dig deeper.

During the Tribulation, we saw the sequence of the seal judgments, the trumpet judgments, and the bowl judgments—each getting worse. The Tribulation comes to an end with the battle—or actually a campaign—called Armageddon (Daniel 11:40–45; Joel 3:9–17; Zechariah 14:1–3; Revelation 16:14–16). Billions of people will die during the Tribulation. Commercial Babylon will be destroyed (Revelation 17–18).

Jesus Christ returns for this final battle of Armageddon and defeats all who stand against Israel. The Antichrist and false prophet are captured and cast forever into the lake of fire. Satan is bound and cast into the bottomless pit for a thousand years.

Please note that when Christ returns to the Mount of Olives, there will be a global earthquake; the whole earth will shake, mountains will be leveled, and islands will vanish. The earth's topography will be drastically changed.

The Millennium begins following the Second Coming of Christ—Jesus will set up His kingdom on earth in Jerusalem (Revelation 20:2–7; Joel 2:21–27; Amos 9:13–14; Zephaniah 3:9–20).

Only saved people will enter the Millennium—both Jews and Gentiles—some with mortal bodies. Resurrected saints shall reign with Christ. Christ will institute a perfect government during this thousand years. Christ will bestow great spiritual blessings and bring physical blessings—including increased longevity. Physical infirmities and illness will be removed.

At the end of the thousand years, Satan will be released and come out to deceive the nations. Satan will gather forces against Jerusalem and make his last stand (Revelation 20:7–8). Satan and his forces face sudden destruction by God, and Satan is thrown into the lake of fire.

The great white throne judgment now takes place, and only the wicked dead are judged and cast into the lake of fire and face eternal torment.

The Millennium now ends, and to get ready for the new heaven and new earth, the earth and universe as we know them must be destroyed by fire and renewed (2 Peter 3:7–13). God does this to get rid of all evil, sin, decay, curses, suffering, death, and Satan's presence.

God now creates a new heaven and new earth. He does this by renovating the heavens and earth, then merges His heaven with a new universe. Isaiah 65:17 reads, "I will create new heavens and a new earth. The former things will not be remembered, nor will they come to mind."

Finally, the new Jerusalem comes down from heaven. This is our new home with our glorified bodies. This city measures approximately fifteen hundred miles in length, width, and height. Please read Revelation 21 for a description of this city. Our human minds cannot comprehend this city, but it is our future home as born-again believers.

There are three main positions taken for the Millennium. I take the pre-millennial position in which Christ returns prior to the thousand-year millennium. All positions are shown at the end of this chapter.

I hope you know Jesus personally and accept Him as your Lord and Savior.

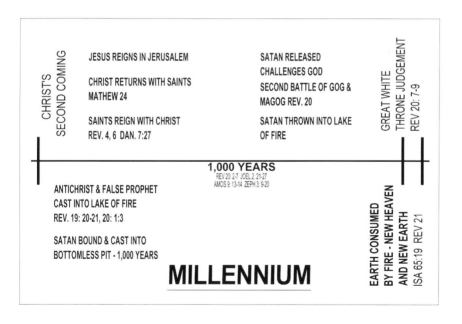

# Millennium

Three positions:

1.  Amillennialism: denial of a literal reign of Christ on the earth.
2.  Pre-millennialism: literal interpretation of scripture. Second Coming of Christ will occur before the thousand-year reign of Christ.
3.  Post-millennialism: whole world will be Christianized and brought to submission to the gospel before return of Christ. Do not believe in literal reign of Christ on earth.

# 19
## Chapter

# How Many People Are Going to Heaven?

How many people are going to heaven? Are you one of them?

Do you know how many people live on earth today? It is 7.7 billion. How many people are in the United States.? Approximately 330 million. That is 4.3 percent of the world population.

How many people, both dead and alive, have ever lived on this earth? That number is estimated to be 107 billion.

What is the population of the top twelve countries? China: 1.42 billion; India: 1.36 billion; United States: 330 million; Indonesia: 267 million; Brazil: 211 million; Pakistan: 202 million; Nigeria: 197 million; Bangladesh: 167 million; Russia: 144 million; Mexico: 131 million; Japan: 127 million; and Ethiopia: 108 million.

You have heard many times that there are two absolutes in life: death and taxes. Let's talk about death. You can look this up: 56 million people die each year worldwide. That is 153,000 each day, 6,390 each hour, and 107 each minute.

In the United States, it is estimated that 7,452 people die each day, which is 310 each hour and 5 each minute. Wow!

Those are shocking numbers, but a reality we do not like to talk about or think about.

Let's now discuss how many people are going to heaven and whether you are one of them.

We must go to the Bible to help answer these questions. Do you believe the Bible to be God's Word to humankind? I hope you do. The Bible is the only source of truth.

Here are some Bible verses and thoughts for you to consider:

John 3:16: "For God so loved the world that he gave his one and only son, that whoever believes in him shall not perish but have eternal life."

John 1:12: "Yet to all who did receive him, to those who believed in his name, he gave the right to become children of God."

John 14:6: "Jesus answered, 'I am the way and the truth and the life. No one comes to the father except through me.'"

Acts 3:19: "Repent, then, and turn to God, so that your sins may be wiped out."

Acts 16:31: "They replied, believe in the Lord Jesus and you will be saved."

Romans 10:9: "If you declare with your mouth, Jesus is lord, and believe in your heart that God raised him from the dead, you will be saved."

Ephesians 2:8–9: "For by grace you have been saved, through faith, and this is not from yourselves, it is the gift of God, not by works, so that no one can boast."

Matthew 7:13–14: "Enter through the narrow gate. For wide is the gate and broad is the road that leads to destruction, and many enter through it. But small is the gate and narrow is the road that leads to life, and only a few find it."

2 Corinthians 13:5: "Examine yourselves to see whether you are in the faith, test yourselves. Do you not realize that Christ Jesus is in you—unless, of course, you fail the test?"

1 Corinthians 2:14: "The person without the spirit does not accept the things that come from the spirit of God but considers them foolishness, and cannot understand them because they are discerned only through the spirit."

Only Jesus can get you to heaven—no deeds, no idols.

Every other religion in the world is based on humankind's efforts to reach God.

Any plan of salvation that is based on the efforts of humankind is doomed to failure.

Salvation is achieved not through good works but by God's grace through Christ.

There is no other way and no other name than Jesus.

God must call you, and you must respond.

Conversion to Christ is a supernatural, divinely wrought miracle.

One who is truly saved will produce works of righteousness—the fruit of the spirit.

So let's address how many are going to heaven. Please know that only God knows the exact number.

Let's take a look at the major religious groups and the number of people in each group.

Christianity: 2.4 billion
Islam: 1.8 billion
Secular/Agnostic/Atheist: 1.1 billion
Hinduism: 1.1 billion
Buddhism: 520 million
Chinese Traditional: 394 million
Ethnic Religions: 300 million
African Traditional: 100 million
And many other groups add up to 7.7 billion people.

Now let's break down the 2.4 billion listed as Christianity.

Catholics: 1.3 billion
Protestants: 920 million
Eastern Orthodox: 270 million
Oriental Orthodox: 86 million
Restoration: 35 million
Independent Catholic: 18 million
And other groups add up to the 2.4 billion.

Now let's look at a few of the major religious groups and list some of their beliefs:

# Islam

*Began in seventh century AD.
*Only one God—Allah.
*Mohammed is a messenger of God.
*Jesus is a prophet.
*Does not accept Trinity or the divinity of Jesus.
*Follows Five Pillars of Islam.
*They pray for return of White Messiah, called the twelfth Imam.
*Everyone outside of Islam is an infidel.

# Hinduism

*Indian religion and way of life.
*Continuous, seemingly eternal existence—reincarnation.
*Ultimate is to reunite with Brahman.
*Circular concept of time.
*Cow is sacred.
*No single founder—no scripture.

# Buddhism

*Buddha taught afterlife and had successful path to nirvana.
*Tradition that focuses on personal spiritual development.
*There is no personal god.
*Ultimate goal is reincarnation; nirvana is the highest state.
*Meditation.
*Heaven not eternal.
*Has five moral precepts.
*Does not worship Buddha but follows his teachings.
*At death, one is reborn into one of six realms, depending on karma.

## Mormons

*Believe in God the Father and His Son, Jesus.
*Nontrinitarian.
*Believe in modern prophets and continuing revelation.
*Having children is essential for the spirit children of God to come to earth.
*Founder Joseph Smith had forty wives and wrote *The Word of Wisdom*, which was inspired revelation from an angel. It is a book of new scripture.
*Allows plural marriage.
*Law of consecration known as united order.

## Jehovah's Witnesses

*God is creator.
*Rejects trinity as unscriptural.
*God is invisible spirit separate from His Son, Jesus.
*Jesus is God's only direct creation; everything else was created through Christ by means of God's power.
*At death, the soul waits—unconscious—for resurrection to an earthly paradise.
*Select few go to heaven: 144,000.

## Catholics

*Based on Nicene Creed—believe in three persons.
*It is the one, holy, catholic, and apostolic church founded by Jesus.
*Bishops are successors of Christ's apostles.
*Pope is successor to St. Peter and has supreme authority.
*Teaches replacement theology, amilleniallism, and no pre-trib rapture.
*Teaches Mary never died; she was sinless and went to heaven without death. Salvation comes through Mary. Assumption is a required belief.

*The pope and priests admit the traditions are not in the Bible but come from the Holy Spirit working through God's church.
*Includes holy sacraments, rosary, works of penance, purgatory, and selling of indulgences.

## Protestants

*Sola fide* (faith alone).
*Sola scriptura* (Bible is infallible).
*Water baptism is not necessary for salvation.
*Includes rapture, seven-year Tribulation, and thousand-year Millennium.
*Trinity: Father, Son, and Holy Spirit.
*Believe in individual salvation from sin, receiving Jesus as their Lord and Savior though faith.

Now to you. How many are going to heaven?

I have read that some Bible scholars believe that only 1 percent (1 in 100) will go to heaven, some say 10 percent (10 in 100), others 25 percent (25 in 100), and the maximum is 33 percent (33 in 100). Knowing what we have learned, I believe we are well under 10 percent.

Using the 10 percent figure, every two minutes, 21 people go to heaven and 193 people goes to Hades or hell worldwide. In the United States, every two minutes, one person goes to heaven and nine people go to Hades or hell.

Please accept Jesus as your Lord and Savior and receive the gift of eternal life in heaven. Don't forget it is you who must make a decision, a yes or no to Jesus. A church, your family, or a friend cannot do that for you.

I want to add that I believe that there are born-again believers within the groups listed under Christianity.

(Information for this chapter came from uri.org, gospelcoalition.org, pewresearch.org, britannica.com, beliefnet.com, religionfacts.com, Christianity.com, jw.org, lds.org, catholic.com, wikipedia.org.)

# 20

## Chapter

# Lucifer

This chapter deals with Lucifer from his creation to his end.

Do you know that we have churches right here in America that worship Satan? Talk about a direct path to hell. The Bible tells us that some people will worship Satan (John 3:19; 2 Corinthians 11:14–15).

Let's talk about Lucifer's creation. God, who is a spirit being, created Lucifer as a spirit in the heavenly realm. Lucifer was "in Eden—the garden of God" (Ezekiel 28:12–19).

Lucifer was created as one of the cherubim and was blameless. He was given a place of rule and authority. He was allowed to travel back and forth between heaven and earth.

Lucifer was created before the earth (Psalm 104:4–5) and existed before the six days of Genesis 1:3–31.

Job 38:4–7 states that all angelic hosts were conscious living witnesses to the initial creation of earth.

Lucifer's existence totally depends on God; he is not self-sufficient, not all-powerful, not all-present, and not all-knowing. His power is limited by God.

Lucifer desired to be like God and elevate his throne above God. His self-esteem and pride took over. As a result, Lucifer and one-third of angels were pushed out of heaven.

After his fall, Lucifer becomes known as Satan. He presently has access to God (Job 1:6) but no longer enters the courts of heaven as one in responsible authority and rule.

God in His timing creates Adam and Eve in the Garden of Eden on this earth. Satan is his fallen state was already present in the garden and spoke to Eve through the intermediary of the serpent.

Satan tempted Adam and Eve, and they fell and sinned against God. Satan was victorious, and sin entered the world and all humankind.

Now Satan even in his fallen state has control over this worldly system. Jesus called Satan "the prince of this world" (John 12:31, 14:30, and 16:11). What is he doing today?

Satan interferes in the affairs of humankind on this present earth.

Satan uses all his power to thwart God's purposes.

Satan still seeks to elevate his throne above God.

Satan is the ultimate source behind every false cult and world religion.

One of the chief works of Satan today is imitating Christianity.

Satan is a master trickster and father of lies (John 8:44; 2 Corinthians 11:14).

Satan does enact evil and cause direct harm on the earth.

Satan does everything he can to tempt individuals and larger groups of people.

Satan leads the world astray, he appeals to humankind's pride, he interferes with the transmission of truth, and he places false believers in the church.

Satan prowls around like a roaring lion looking for someone to devour (1 Peter 5:8).

Satan attacks us by using the ungodly world to stir up fleshly lust within us that tempts us to sin.

Satan deceives us with worldly wisdom as opposed to God's truth.

Satan attacks by using false Christians to mislead using a false gospel.

Satan sometimes physically inflicts us or our loved ones with sickness, crime, tragedy, and persecution.

Let's look at situations and things happening in today's world that are associated with Satan:

Killings and muggings; suicides; divorce; throwaway kids; abortions; pornography; prostitution; sex trafficking; lesbian and gay marriages; alcohol use; illicit drugs; medical and recreational marijuana; love of money; witchcraft; racism; idols; cults; prayer out of schools; taking God out of everything; humanism; Illuminati; and there is more you can add to this list.

Let me get real specific with an example. We hear of this often in today's news. It is a book written by Saul Alinsky called *Rules for Radicals*. In it, he lists thirteen rules for using subversive tactics for defeating the opposition. It has become the playbook of the left and far left.

I bring this up because Saul Alinsky dedicated this book to Satan.

God is allowing Satan to have limited powers on this earth today. Before we discuss the future of Satan during the Tribulation and the demise of Satan after the Millennium, let's have some good news.

God had a plan to crush Satan's power, and that is Jesus; the cross of Christ has already won the victory. Colossians 1:13 tells us that those who believe are "delivered from the power of darkness and conveyed into the kingdom of the son of God's love."

Satan has no more authority over those who are in Christ. Please know the only power that is guaranteed to defeat Satan every time is the power of the Holy Spirit residing within a believer who is equipped with the armor of God (Ephesians 6:11–17; 2 Corinthians 10:4).

Satan is very aware that Jesus died on the cross to pay the penalty for our sins. He is working overtime since he knows his time is limited.

Let's discuss Satan's final defeat. During the upcoming seven-year Tribulation, Satan will inhabit the Antichrist (2 Thessalonians 2:4). During the last half of the Tribulation, God throws Satan down to earth, his final expulsion from heaven; he fell as lightning from heaven (Luke 10:18; Revelation 12:7–9).

Satan is defeated at Christ's Second Coming at the end of the Tribulation. God cast him into the bottomless pit during the thousand-year Millennium (Revelation 20:2). At the end of the Millennium,

Satan is let loose and defeated for the last time—the final war. God then casts Satan into the eternal lake of fire (Revelation 20:7–10).

Do you know God personally? Have you accepted Christ as your Lord and Savior? If not, please accept Christ and put on the whole armor of God so you can have victory over Satan.

# 21

## Chapter

# You

How old are you? Are you part of the Greatest Generation born before 1946? Are you a baby boomer born between 1946 and 1964? Are you part of Generation X born between 1965 and 1980? Are you a millennial born between 1981 and 1996? Or are you part of Generation Z born between 1997 and today?

No matter what your age, I have a question for you. When you are all alone, no talking, no music, no TV, no iPhones, no computers—just plain quiet—what do you think about? Where does your mind go?

Is it family, wife and kids, church, food, your phone, sports, clothes, money, porn, lust (which means a very strong sexual desire for someone)? Just what do you think about?

Let me ask this: do you ever think about God? Did you know that you were created in God's image and likeness? (Genesis 1:27). Genesis 1:26 and 2:7 state that humans are unique among all God's creation, having both a material body and an immortal soul/spirit.

By the way, you are one of a kind. You are the only one like you. Out of 7.7 billion people on earth today—or of the approximately 110 billion people since God created humankind—you are the one! You are it!

We are all born into sin because of Adam and Eve. They fell into sin when tempted by Satan. Even in our fallen state, God endows part of His spirit into us at birth. Romans 2:14–15 tells us that our conscience also bears witness. The human conscience is a law written on the heart by the Lord so that each of us innately knows that lying, stealing, murder, and other sins are wrong.

We are also born with a free will. God allows us to choose and make decisions. Since we have a sinful nature, if one chooses not to follow God, here is a sequence that will likely happen.

If you succumb to more and more sinful desires, over time that little part of God's spirit will leave you. Your conscience will become "seared with a hot iron," meaning you will no longer care about the consequences of your sin and merely live life seeking to satisfy your lusts (Romans 1:18–22).

Continuing the descent into depravity, Romans 1:18–28 talks about your "foolish heart" being "darkened." If you continue to deny God's existence and thus His authority over humanity, you will fall deeper into imagining what is right or wrong, and you will become your own God and authority of your life.

Now to the final step. The denial of God and His authority leads to idolatry and sinful lust. God will give you "over to a reprobate mind, to those things which are not convenient" (Romans 1:28). God removes His remaining influence and you become a reprobate—fully turned over to your own wicked desires. What that means is that you are wretched and good for nothing.

I hope you are not on this path of destruction and total depravity. Just look at the world around us; it is very concerning. Satan is on the winning side at this time.

There is good news. God has a wonderful plan for you and me. That plan includes God's Son, Jesus, going to the cross, shedding His blood, and taking on Himself all of our sins.

Back to my original question—do you think about God in your quiet times? God's desire is that during your lifetime, you will accept Jesus as your Lord and Savior. Why did God create us? God created us for His pleasure and so that we, as His creation, would have the pleasure of knowing Him. Our ultimate purpose is to glorify God.

Is God calling you? Have you felt God tugging on your heart, soul, and spirit? Please yield to Him and become a brand-new creation.

# 22
## Chapter

# Is Hell Real?

Is hell real? Absolutely.

When was the last time you heard a sermon preached about hell? The reality is that hell is one of the least talked about scriptural teachings from the pulpit. And why do pastors shy away from the topic? It might scare people, so if it gets presented, it is watered down as if it is not a real place. Let's get real—it is definitely not a message for any preacher who wants fame or notoriety. In today's world, the preacher must keep the people happy and feeling good so the money will keep coming in.

Before we jump into what the Bible says about hell, let's list some objections we hear today from within and outside of the church that hell cannot be true in the first place.

The first is universalism—a belief that all will get saved.

The second is hell is only temporary—eventually all will get out.

The third is annihilation—people in hell will just cease to be or die.

The fourth is hell has no value—hell was not for people but just for the devil and his demons.

And lastly hell is life on this earth and we live it daily.

Who created hell? Did you guess Satan? It was God. God created hell for Satan and his angels (Matthew 25:41). God did not create hell for humankind, but we fell to sin in the Garden of Eden, and God then had to accommodate humankind in hell. Hell is the eternal home for all sin and rebellion. The Bible teaches that hell is a place of sorrow, weeping, torture, and torment.

Where is hell? There are various theories on its location. The traditional view is that it is located in the center of earth. Another view is it is located in outer space in a black hole. And one more—the earth itself will be the "lake of fire" spoken of in Revelation 20:10–15.

Here is the answer—the Bible does not tell us the geological or cosmological location of hell. Only God knows. I believe it is located in another realm or dimension that humans cannot comprehend. The important thing is to avoid going there.

What is hell like? Here are a few characteristics:

- place of eternal torment (Revelation 20)
- place of weeping and gnashing of teeth (Matthew 13)
- place of everlasting punishment (Matthew 25)
- place of lake of fire (Revelation 20)
- place of bottomless pit (Luke 8)

- place of wicked demons (2 Peter 2)

- place of no return (Luke 16)

Did you know there are five compartments in hell? Let's review.

The first compartment is Tartarus. This is where the fallen angels are kept until they are judged by God and cast into the lake of fire (2 Peter 2:4; Jude 16).

The second compartment is Abraham's bosom. This is where the righteous dead of the Old Testament were kept. There was no torment or suffering in Abraham's bosom. It was simply a place of holding until the death and resurrection of Jesus. At the resurrection of Jesus, Abraham's bosom was emptied and is now located in heaven. All the righteous dead were set free and resurrected (Matthew 27:51–53). Please read Luke 16:19–31.

The third compartment is Hades or Sheol. Hades is the Greek form of the word *hell*. Sheol is the Hebrew word for hell. This is the place for the wicked after death. When sinners die, their soul and spirit go to this place of torment.

The fourth compartment is the abyss. The abyss is also known as the bottomless pit. This is where Satan will be bound for a thousand years during the reign of Christ on earth (Revelation 20:1–7). This is also from where locust-like scorpion creatures will ascend upon the earth and torment humankind for five months during the seven-year Tribulation (Revelation 9:1–11).

The fifth compartment is the lake of fire. This is the eternal home of all sin and rebellion. All who are judged at the white throne judgment of God will be assigned to the lake of fire (Revelation 20:11–15). All people who do not know Jesus personally will be there for eternity.

Now let's get down to the bottom line. Who goes to hell? The Bible is clear as to who goes to hell:

- the wicked (Psalm 9:17)

- the harlot or prostitute (Proverbs 7:5–27, 9:13–18, 2:18)

- those with a lack of knowledge (Isaiah 5:13–14)

- those who have transgressed against God (Isaiah 66:24)

- the fearful, unbelieving, abominable, idolaters, murderers, sorcerers, and all liars (Revelation 21:8)

And if you dig deeper in the Bible, you will find others destined for hell.

In conclusion, none of us escape death. We are all appointed once to die (Hebrews 9:27). You get to choose where you will go upon death—heaven or hell. Jesus came to save us from hell. I do not want you to go to a literal hell. Accept Jesus as your Lord and Savior.

# 23

## Chapter

# The Antichrist

Do you know who the Antichrist is? You need to know about him so you will understand last day events.

In today's world, the Antichrist is mentioned more often than Christ. The prefix *anti* can mean the exact opposite or it can mean another, replaced, or instead of.

His name comes from the apostle John. 1 John 2:18 reads, "Dear children, this is the last hour, and as you have heard that the Antichrist is coming, even now many antichrists have come. This is how we know it is the last hour." In fact, verse 19 tells us that some antichrists went out from the church. I will tell you they are still in the church today.

The Bible tells us that the Antichrist is the beast (Revelation 13:1–4) and he is a Gentile (Revelation 17:15). He comes from the revived Roman Empire. Daniel 9:26 tells us he is the prince of the Roman Empire.

The Antichrist could actually be alive and living on earth today. When does the Antichrist break onto the scene to begin his worldwide campaign?

I believe the rapture of the saints, the true believers in Christ, is the event that triggers the unveiling of the Antichrist.

After the rapture all hell breaks loose on this earth. There is a gap of a few years between the rapture and the beginning of the seven-year Tribulation.

It is during the gap period that Jesus opens the first seal (Revelation 6:1–2) in which a white horse and rider appear. This is the Antichrist! Please read 2 Thessalonians 2:3–4; Daniel 9:24–27; and Matthew 24.

The Tribulation officially begins when the Antichrist confirms a peace treaty with Israel and with Death and Sheol (Daniel 9:27; Isaiah 28:15,18).

At the midpoint of the seven-year Tribulation, the Antichrist breaks the treaty, enters into the Jewish temple, and makes himself God.

His destiny is this: the Armageddon war takes place at the end of the Tribulation in which God defeats the Antichrist and his armies. At this point, God throws the Antichrist and the false prophet into the lake of fire: their eternal damnation.

Satan, who is the ultimate Antichrist (Isaiah 14:12–14), is thrown into the abyss during the Millennium: a thousand-year period. After the Millennium, Satan is let loose one last time, is defeated in his final war, and then is thrown into the eternal lake of fire (Revelation 19:20).

Here is the bottom line: I don't want you to meet the Antichrist! My desire is that you know Jesus personally.

All born-again believers will be raptured when Christ returns for His church, and we will be with Jesus in heaven during the gap period and the seven-year Tribulation.

Here is what you will miss:

The Antichrist will intimidate world leaders.

He will be reviled, a political animal, smooth and charming.

He will be admired and worshipped. He will become an actual object of worship.

He will emerge from obscurity (Daniel 7:8, 24), and he will be honored by governments as an apparent savior of humankind. He will become a leader of the one-world political and economic system.

He will acquire "authority over every tribe and people and tongue and nation" (Revelation 13:7).

He will be the last great human emperor.

He will blaspheme God and persecute believers.

He will be sexually perverted, likely a homosexual (Daniel 11:37).

He will be a genius in intellect, commerce, war, speech, and politics.

I pray that you will accept Jesus as your Lord and Savior.

# 24

## Chapter

# Guardian Angels

Do you have a guardian angel? We will attempt to answer that once we learn about angels. Angels are real; the Bible mentions them 273 times. God created Lucifer and all the angels before He created the physical universe. Job 38:4–7 tells us that the morning stars sang together and all the angels shouted for joy when God laid the earth's foundation.

Who are these angels? What does the Bible say?

Angels are spirit beings and do not have true physical bodies—no flesh or bones (Luke 24:39).

There are three types of angels mentioned in the Bible. They are the cherubim (Genesis 3:24); the seraphim (Isaiah 6:2); and the living creatures or hosts (Ezekiel 1:5–14; Revelation 4:6–8).

Angels do not marry (Matthew 22:30).

Now I will tread on thin ice—most of us grew up thinking all angels have wings. Not quite true—most angels do not have wings. There are some exceptions though (Isaiah 6:2–7; Ezekiel 1:4–28; Genesis 3:24; and Revelation 4:6–8).

With this one I will likely break through the ice and flounder. Angels when mentioned in the Bible are always in the masculine gender and always dressed as human males (Genesis 18:2,16; Ezekiel 9:2).

The only named angels in the Bible are Michael, Gabriel, and Lucifer.

Angels can take on mundane human form (Genesis 19:1–4).

Angels have intelligence, emotions, and wills.

Angels were created as an order of creatures higher than humans.

Their knowledge is limited, but they have the ability to reason.

Angels are finite creatures and limited to one place at one time.

There are also killer angels: "that night the angel of the Lord went out and put to death a hundred and eighty-five thousand in the Assyrian camp" (2 Kings 19:35).

What are the functions of angels? Let's list a few.

They are messengers (Acts 7:52–53; Luke 1:11–20).

They protect certain people (Daniel 6:20–23, Daniel 12:1; 2 Kings 6:13–17).

They are "ministering spirits sent to serve those who will inherit salvation" (Hebrews 1:14).

They worship God around His throne (Revelation 5:11–14, 22:8–9; Isaiah 6:2–3).

They watch over us physically, morally, and spiritually (Psalm 91:11).

They do God's will (Psalm 103:20).

They praise God; worship God; rejoice in what God does; serve God; appear before God; are instruments of God's judgments; bring answers to prayers; aid in winning people to Christ; observe Christian order, work and suffering; encourage in times of danger; and care for righteous at time of death.

A word of warning—we are told not to worship angels (Revelation 19:9–10, 22:9). Revelation 22:8–9 tells us that holy angels refuse to be worshipped. Do not focus on angels and do not pray to them.

I have to mention that there are fallen angels. Lucifer, who became Satan, brought one-third of the angels with him when he fell (Revelation 12:3–9; Hebrews 12:22). Fallen angels work for Satan (Galatians 1:8; Colossians 2:18). Demons, who are evil angels, are either free to roam or are bound in chains in the abyss (2 Peter 2:4).

Here is one to ponder: "Do not forget to show hospitality to strangers, for by so doing some people have shown hospitality to angels without knowing it" (Hebrews 13:2). That could be you!

Now back to the original question. Do you have a guardian angel watching over you? Let's look at Matthew 18:10: "See that you do not despise one of these little ones, for I tell you that their angels in Heaven always see the face of my Father in Heaven." The "little ones" could be believers or could be little children. It is likely we do not have an assigned angel for every individual. There is no direct biblical support, but it may exist.

But please know that angels are watching over you. I pray that you know Jesus as your Lord and Savior.

# Next Steps

I hope you have enjoyed reading this book. I hope it has been an inspirational, challenging, and thought-provoking read. I pray that the Holy Spirit has inspired you to dig deeper into God's Word.

I would be remiss not to leave you with these next steps. World events are converging quickly. Here are some ways you can have a personal relationship with God:

1. I want you to be one of a very few who enter heaven. You can have that blessed hope of spending eternity in heaven. I want you to know Jesus personally by placing your faith in Him.
2. If God is knocking at your door, be ready, open the door, and let Him in. You can do this by praying the sinner's prayer. God will not force you to accept Jesus as Savior—you must decide (1 Timothy 1:12).
3. Sinner's prayer: "God, I admit I am a sinner and ask for forgiveness of my sins. I want to ask your Son, Jesus, to come into my life and be my Lord and Savior." Read Romans 10:9–10.
4. Faith comes by hearing, and hearing by the Word of God (Romans 10:17). Faith requires three things: conviction, trust in God, and obedience.

5. Regeneration is the renewing of the heart and mind and being born again, which means "born from above."
6. The next step is to begin a life dedicated to Jesus Christ, our Lord and Savior. Start your journey of becoming more Christlike. It is not easy—it takes a lot of hard work.
7. Please find a Bible-believing church in your area and consider being baptized as an act of obedience and to let people know of your commitment.

# References

Below is a list all the authors, the Bible, and websites that have had a huge impact on my spiritual life and have been instrumental in the making of this book.

Bible (NIV)
David Jeremiah
Paul McGuire
David Reagan
Gary Stearman
Bill Salus
Mark Hitchcock
Robert Cornuke
Billy Crone
Ryan Pitterson
Jack Langford
Jan Markell
Andy Woods
Steven Dill
Ken Johnson
Don Perkins
Larry Ollison

L. A. Marzulli
Tom Hughes
Dan Goodwin
Ron Cantor
John MacArthur
Gotquestions.org
Https://ipfs.io/ipfs
Worldpopulationreview.com

# About the Author

James L. McClain is a semiretired structural engineer and has enjoyed a great forty-six-year career. He asked God to be part of his life years ago through His Son, Jesus.

Now he devotes his time to God, his wife, taking care of two homes, and a little woodworking. He is a past private pilot with an instrument ticket (the reason for the plane logo on the website and this book cover).

He loves studying and digging deep into God's Word and has a special love for eschatology.

He wants to share Christ.

James L. McClain, Professional Engineer
BSCE, MSCE
Member of Chi Epsilon Honorary Fraternity
Registered in twenty-two states over career

Printed in the United States
By Bookmasters